Map of the City of Seattle

showing main thoroughfares and some places of interest

SCALE IN MILES

for Donald P. Schlegel –
in appreciation of your visit
to Seattle and to the
University of Washington
May 1982   Victor Steinbrueck

Seattle
Cityscape #2

UNIVERSITY OF WASHINGTON PRESS   SEATTLE AND LONDON

Seattle
Cityscape #2

BY VICTOR STEINBRUECK

Library of Congress Cataloging in Publication Data

Steinbrueck, Victor.
  Seattle cityscape # 2.

   1. Seattle—Description—Views. I. Title.
F899.S443S75   917.97'77   73–15964
ISBN 0–295–95293–8

A little more than an hour from Seattle is the wilderness that was Seattle and has always been close to its heart. The natural areas are rapidly receding, but they are still there. If enlightened public interest can prevail, these sacred places will not be lost to commercial uses. One such area is the valley of Boulder River, one of the finest remaining unlogged but unprotected areas in the state. This is the last low-elevation virgin forest close to Puget Sound and is proposed for inclusion in the Whitehorse Wilderness Area. Accessible only on foot, it is located in the Cascade Mountains near Darrington, just north of Mount Pilchuck. Nearness to woods and mountains remains one of Seattle's most attractive qualities.

Image of a City

All of my life I have been exploring and looking at this city called Seattle. I cannot name any place here that I have not watched change, grow, or decay during the last half century. And yet I do not know the city completely—nor can anyone. In the beginning, my childish curiosity led me to discover life and places and things with Seattle and its hinterland as my whole world, on foot, by bicycle, by streetcar, and sometimes in our family's old Dodge touring car. I still have an abiding curiosity to see what is happening everywhere within my reach, and I deeply yearn for the changes to enrich the lives of people of Seattle, to be good for the whole city.

I have lived in Georgetown, Mount Baker, Beacon Hill, West Seattle, Alki, Denny Blaine, the Central area, the University district, and Capitol Hill. As a youth I assiduously photographed Seattle views, buildings, back alleys, and people. When I decided to become an architect, I took up pencil and brush in order to learn to draw as well as to know better the world around me. Since then I have continued to learn by drawing, and by the same means I have been trying to tell something to the people of Seattle. Perhaps I might be called a graphic environmental propagandist.

Daily movement about the city continues to be a fascinating exploration and rediscovery as I have studied the Puget Sound region's buildings and the city's form as well as its human uses. My image of the city is a multidimensional one of sight, sound, smell, and feel experienced in time, movement, and place. City changes are a never-ending source of interest, sometimes pleasant, too often sad. Some memorable places no longer exist—the historic old Kalmar Hotel which stood in the path of the freeway, old Luna swimming pool at Duwamish, the farmer's garden in South Park where now industry grows, or the theatrical old Meany Hall on the University of Washington campus.

Every building and street, every bridge and highway, every man-made element, whether beautiful, mediocre, or ugly, is part of the city and conveys a message about its people. Every hill and every tree is also part of the city, as is every utility pole and overhead wire. And each and every asphalt parking lot or concrete garage that has replaced a livable building acts as a blighting cancer destroying the city's quality. All of these urban forms, together with the natural setting, significantly express the city's character.

When I sketched the first *Seattle Cityscape* in 1962, I wanted the citizens to look at their city; to see how it was put together, how it fitted or misfitted the land and water. I was trying to encourage awareness of the quality—or lack of quality—of the man-made environment. At that time I wrote: "Because of a particular combination of favorable conditions, Seattle is more than just a city; it is a very special unique place. These favorable characteristics are its unsurpassed natural setting, combining greenery, hills, and water, and its proximity to the country and natural waterways; the pleasant, changing, temperate climate; and the adventurous, freedom-loving people who live here. The people have made and are making the city, and it in turn exercises its influences upon their destinies." A good city ought to have well-defined and diversified cultural, social, and economic resources that are expressed in the physical reality of its layout and form. Seattle contains many of these elements, although appropriate and harmonious potentials have too often yielded to avaricious mediocrity or just poor taste, as in every American city. Our economic system surely makes it difficult not to place private gains above civic welfare and betterment.

There are good things taking place in Seattle, but there is much for architects, planners, and city-watchers to worry about. There is not much really high quality new architecture in civic or private buildings. Most residential buildings have been for profit rather than for people. Not since the first decade of this century, when the park and boulevard system was established, has Seattle enjoyed enlightened and visionary civic leadership capable of favorably influencing the overall quality of its environment. In recent years, considerable capital improvements have been taking place as the result of the Forward Thrust bond issue of 1967. But while the design quality of some of the individual projects has been high, there has been a serious lack of effective planning and coordination. There have also been a few architectural monstrosities in both public and private development. Nevertheless, many of these sketches show that Seattle's truly unsurpassed natural setting has thus far withstood the onslaught of short-sighted "economic progress," although too many locations have suffered irreparable physical injustices.

In the first *Seattle Cityscape,* I hoped to encourage a better understanding of architecture, especially in relation to its time and place, to expose the reader to the flow of building styles of this region. This second *Cityscape,* while it is in no sense intended to be a complete guide to Seattle, comes closer, I believe, to enabling the reader to look at the city through my eyeglasses and penpoint. The drawings are larger, and they give more of a look at the overall picture of the city—more townscape, more streets, more atmosphere. Some of the drawings from the earlier book have been included, as well as several from a series done for the *Seattle Post-Intelligencer,* but reproduced full-size and updated to include changes, especially in the downtown skyline. Most of the sketches are new. Ranging from residential streets, parks, freeways, and waterways to the cruelest and most sterile downtown office buildings and parking garages, they demonstrate the range of urban situations that is Seattle.

Seattle Cityscape #2, like its predecessor, is a sketchbook by an architect, an effort to communicate one concerned observer's idea of the city. It does not attempt to give answers, but, by showing the way things are, it does indicate problems; and perhaps the delineation of some of the city's positive qualities does suggest solutions. Seattle's topography and natural elements remain its most precious as well as its most exploited assets. Realistic hope for the future depends upon public and private awareness, concern, and civic involvement, with a real commitment to human values above material considerations. It is to this commitment, and the vital part that it must play in building a good and livable city for our children, our friends, and ourselves, that this book is dedicated.

As one approaches the central business district from the north on the Seattle Freeway, the massing of new commercial landmarks comes impressively into view past landlocked, active Lake Union. Beyond Elliott Bay, the headland of West Seattle can be seen, along with a glimpse of Puget Sound and the distant Olympic Mountains on a clear day. The Space Needle's unique form pinpoints Seattle Center with its collection of recreational buildings.

South from residential Queen Anne Hill, the panorama over Seattle Center is surely one of the most splendid views of any city in the world. Seattle Center is the city's heritage from the Century 21 World's Fair of 1962. Crowned by the omnipresent Space Needle, the entertainment complex of the Arena, the Opera House, the Exhibition Hall, and the Playhouse stretches along Mercer Street, with the aluminum tent-roofed Coliseum dominating the western section of the civic center. The tall buildings of downtown compose most attractively between water and hillside, often with the glorious soft-colored backdrop of Mount Rainier adding to the scene.

One of Seattle's enduring attributes is the many views available from so many locations. Yet there is relatively minimal provision for lookout places from which to enjoy scenic splendors. This view is from a private yard. More lookouts for views must become a civic program.

10

In 1962 I wrote, "Seen from west of the bay at a small lookout park on the tip of Duwamish Head, the central business district of Seattle provides a thrilling panorama by day and by night." Of course what I wrote is still true, and this is a great place to watch the rapidly changing skyline as new commercial high-rise towers are added. Economic progress is changing Seattle's character and image, as is evident from here as well as on downtown streets and in the suburbs. From this location, in little more than a century, has been seen the transition from a completely forested virgin wilderness sparsely inhabited by native American Indians to a typical steel, concrete, and glass twentieth-century American city. The fine natural setting still offers the potential for Seattle to become one of the beautiful cities of the world if the leadership of people of unselfish civic vision can be implemented. If Seattle is to become great, it will only be because of the quality of life it offers its citizens, and not because of economic growth alone.

The approach to historic Pioneer Square from First Avenue South reveals the location of the beginnings of downtown Seattle. It was here that Henry Yesler's lumber mill was located in 1853 to form the one-industry economic basis for the young town. Most of the present buildings were built immediately after the fire of 1889, which burned out all of Seattle's downtown buildings. The brick and stone buildings are usually Romanesque or Gothic Revival in the Victorian manner of the times. Their proximity to such contemporary office structures as the Norton and Seattle–First National Bank buildings provides a dramatic contrast not unfavorable to the older buildings. The Pioneer Square and Skid Road areas to the south are prospering again as the result of historic preservation assistance.

One of the nicest things that has happened to Seattle in the last fifty years is the restoration of Pioneer Square as a lovely cobblestoned park designed by Jones and Jones, landscape architects. Much credit goes to the benefactor, Jim Casey, who founded United Parcel Service in this area in 1907. The Pioneer Building, built in 1889, architect Elmer Fisher, is one of the best examples of Victorian Romanesque Revival architecture and has been awaiting sympathetic restoration and use for many years. Other buildings surrounding the square offer rich potential for appropriate and profitable use as more and better shops, restaurants, and galleries find the historic district to be an attractive location. Downtown residential accommodation is the greatest need to help breathe life into Pioneer Square as well as all of downtown.

The view up the skid road, now called Yesler Way, through Pioneer Square is a dramatic one framed by vintage buildings on all sides. The Smith Tower dominates as it was intended to do since its erection in 1914, when it was built to help anchor Seattle's downtown to this end of the business district. As new high-rise towers are built nearby, the unique form of the old tower looks better and better. The triangular "sinking ship" garage violates the view and is esthetically incompatible with its neighbors. It has been the subject of controversy since before it was built, and hope remains that it will be removed, or at least obscured by landscaping. One of the attractive aspects of Pioneer Square is the fact that it is enjoyed by people from all strata of life, including native American Indians, who often meet here.

Café Amstelredamme

David Ishii-Bookseller

Clodalls

Tastefully and imaginatively restored under the guidance of architect Ralph Anderson, the former Grand Central Hotel (South Main Street and First Avenue South) is enjoying a posh existence with its many luxurious shops and offices. Rehabilitation of this building has helped to give economic stability to historic preservation. As part of Seattle's Skid Road area, it symbolizes, through its change from a very low-income hotel to this "upgraded" use, both interest in the city's past and civic disregard for our least favored citizens, the displaced Skid Road denizens. Many small businesses throughout the historic district are bringing a unique and colorful quality to this part of downtown.

As sketched in 1965 before the Pioneer Square district had been "saved," First Avenue South was the hangout and shelter for homeless men—seasonal laborers, old-age pensioners, alcoholics, and "urban nomads"—the problem people of our society who have been easy to ignore. Now that economic and cultural progress has pushed most of them elsewhere, the human problem remains unsolved, although it has become more noticeable as various sectors of society rub shoulders on First Avenue or on the benches in the new parks. The block of buildings on the west side of First Avenue South below South Washington Street is an example of unostentatious but fairly consistent brick buildings that form a group more impressive than the individual buildings. Its lack of high style is made up for by harmony in material, scale, and size.

The first location of significant historic restoration in Seattle was Occidental Avenue South between Jackson Street and South Main Street. Private enterprise was responsible for urban renewal in the best sense of the phrase, with entrepreneurs Richard White and architect Ralph Anderson acting as the moving forces. Largely through their consistent and persistent efforts, and with help from some civic groups, the street was boulevarded in front of the buildings they had carefully restored, thereby setting an example for similar development of the entire district. The view to the north is an intriguing one, exposing the city's architectural history from the early Pioneer Building to the overbearing, dominant, black Sea-First Building.

First Avenue north from Madison Street is one of the most interesting and active streets in all of the city, although not a favorite haunt of the elite. It contains a worthy collection of historic buildings not yet publicly recognized. First Avenue has always been the place where the action is. It is the honky-tonk, colorful street of signs, old and new, screaming and sometimes wailing for attention to its variety of small shops, taverns, run-down hotels, and diverse services. This is the bottom of the city, completely vulnerable to redevelopment except for the protection its uncouthness affords to the profit-seeking entrepreneur.

21

Although historically it was always known as Chinatown, this neighborhood is now called the International District through some sort of "city lovely" effort. The population is international, or more correctly interracial, since the district encompasses the old center and residence of the Chinese community, many years of association with the Japanese, the homes of many older Filipinos, and a large concentration of Blacks. Special ethnic stores and restaurants serve these people and the rest of the city as well, adding a special cosmopolitan flavor to be enjoyed and cherished. The Seattle Freeway construction isolated the area. Now redevelopment for more profitable commercial purposes threatens to disrupt the life of the community. Some residential hotels have been closed without replacement housing being available.

Less than one hundred years of commercial development, known as progress, have produced this change in downtown Seattle. The sketches are both from the same location, looking south on Second Avenue from the vicinity of Pike Street; the earlier is the view in 1878.

Bird's-eye view of Seattle and environs, 1891, eighteen months after the Great Fire (lithograph by Augustus Koch, courtesy of Northwest Collection, University of Washington Libraries)

Proposed Central Waterfront Park

26

Judging from the crowds on a typical sunny Sunday, Seattle's central waterfront has changed from a working waterfront to a walking waterfront. The appeal of the water, the view, the marine activities, and the old shipping piers, which are being exploited to the utmost by all sorts of fashionable new shops and restaurants catering to tourists and visitors from Bellevue, combine to form a lively, heterogeneous experience which surely will be enhanced by the new waterfront proposal from the architects Bumgardner Partnership, shown on the opposite page below. Unfortunately there is no easy pedestrian connection to the booming development north at Pier 70 (architects Harader, Mebust and Schorr), to the Pike Place Market, to the main downtown shopping district, or to Chinatown. Planning has not progressed that far in Seattle. While this development is very attractive architecturally and commercially, it is unfortunate that it could not have been located where it would have enhanced existing retail areas—for instance, in the Westlake Park.

From Yesler Way across the Seattle Freeway, the city's "governmental center" appears to be an architectural mess—an impression confirmed by closer observation of the main buildings. The chaotic mediocrity of the Seattle Municipal Building or "City Hall" (1960) and the adjacent King County Administration Building (1969) is apparent. Since buildings are inevitably the expression of the forces that produce them, these examples are revealing as to the quality of the responsible local governments. The nearby freeway contributes noise and air pollution to the already unpleasing visual environment.

Looking north on Fourth Avenue from James Street invites comparison between the timid, commonplace Seattle Municipal Building and the overpowering Seattle–First National Bank Building, with its status-bestowing sculpture by Henry Moore and its competitive new neighbor, the Bank of California Center. From the relative stature and dominance of the three buildings, it appears that private finance and commercial development are more important facets of the city than are public service and governance. Moore's bronze *Vertebrae* is part of a significant modern art collection that has been incorporated into the otherwise urbanely sterile Sea-First Building.

29

South on Third Avenue from the vicinity of Union Street, the Sea-First Building continues to dominate the cityscape, forming a backdrop for the handsomest high-rise building in Seattle, the Northern Life Tower (now called the Seattle Tower), built in 1929. Its form and color are suggestive of the rugged nearby mountain peaks. The new Financial Center building also looms heavily into the scene.

This part of Third Avenue is still honky-tonk and down-to-earth human, with taverns, restaurants, pool rooms, and a risque movie house which have been spared the benefits of redevelopment in recent years. On the opposite corner is the mundane main Post Office, which replaced an ornate and colorful old Renaissance Revival building in the 1950s.

At Third Avenue and Pike Street, the scene has changed little since 1960, having kept its strength because of the retail attraction of the two big "ten-cent" stores. Public transit is busiest here, contributing to the general activity. Pike Street, along with Pine Street one block to the north, forms the connecting pedestrian path between First Avenue and the Pike Place Market, and Fourth and Fifth avenues with their more prestigious shops and important department stores. The connection could be strengthened by better weather protection, more street-level attractions, and reduction of conflicting automobile traffic. Nothing altruistic has ever been done to improve the quality of enjoyment for shoppers in these vital retail areas, which are directly in competition with the newer, automobile-oriented shopping centers in outlying areas. The Woolworth Building is a fine example of the Art Deco style of the twenties.

Orient AIRLINE

32

This view down Fourth Avenue from University Street, showing the pedestrian skybridge between the Olympic Hotel and the new Financial Center building, may be a look into the future. The architects for University Properties, which is developing the downtown property owned by the University of Washington, are proposing that pedestrians be relocated to a higher level above the streets with many skybridges connecting the various buildings. This solution will avoid conflict with the automobile, but pedestrian street activity will be diverted and divided, and it is unlikely that the total scheme of raising all the people downtown to another level can ever be accomplished. This concept has already fallen into disfavor elsewhere. The buildings are very competently handled; they do not, however, offer any attraction or visual enjoyment to the shopper or city wanderer.

South from the Bon Marche department store at Fourth Avenue and Pine Street is the location of the much-disputed proposed Westlake Park. The fulcrum of middle-class downtown shopping is here, and the established interests are reluctant to risk changing anything, while less selfish city lovers hope to humanize downtown by lessening automobile traffic and developing a pedestrian open space. The mix of architecture of the 1920s and 1930s is pleasantly scaled and rather harmonious because of the eclectic ornamentation and not excessive building size. Typical of many American cities in its ordinariness, it is surely more acceptable than the aggressive ugliness and sterility of some more recent developments.

Fifth Avenue from University Street north includes some of the best urban architecture in Seattle. Much of the work came from the office of architect R. C. Reamer, including the fine Skinner Building, which houses the Fifth Avenue Theatre—an elegant moving-picture palace of the late 1920s, beautifully decorated in Chinese style. There are no projecting signs on the stores, and yet they do a brisk business. The next block to the north becomes another hodgepodge of miscellaneous commercialism with a new Peoples National Bank Building rising where once stood the Blue Mouse Theatre. The ostentatious cylindrical Washington Plaza Hotel visually terminates the street, which changes direction at that point.

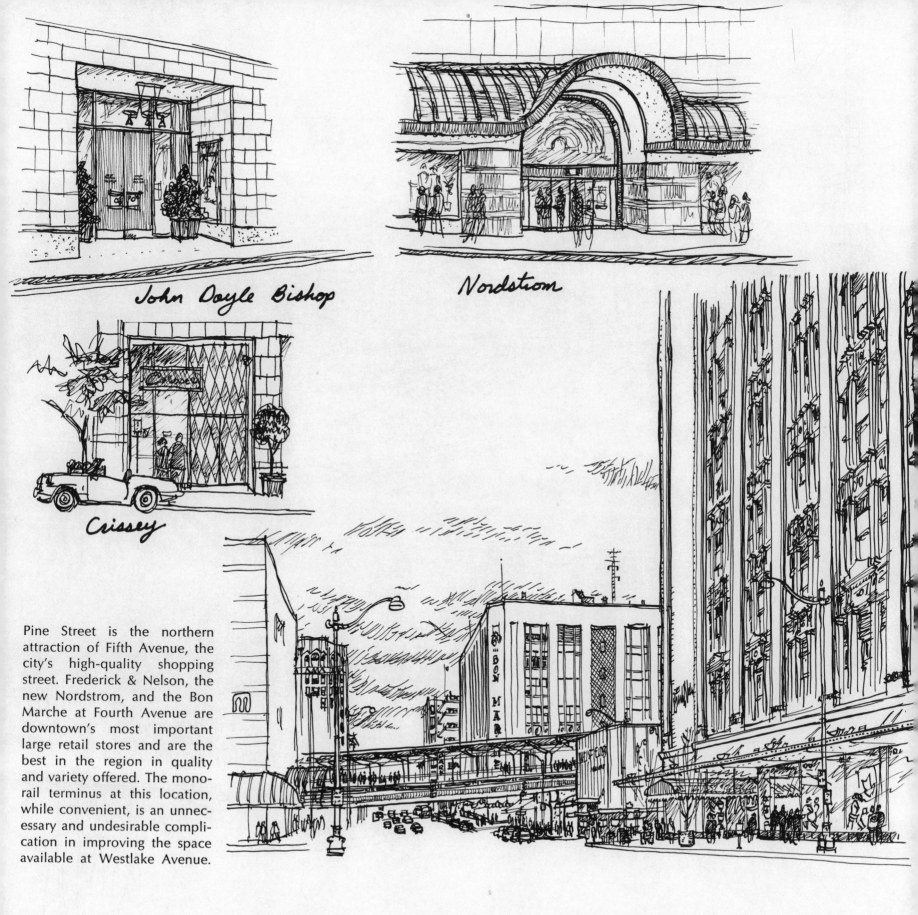

John Doyle Bishop

Nordstrom

Crissey

Pine Street is the northern attraction of Fifth Avenue, the city's high-quality shopping street. Frederick & Nelson, the new Nordstrom, and the Bon Marche at Fourth Avenue are downtown's most important large retail stores and are the best in the region in quality and variety offered. The monorail terminus at this location, while convenient, is an unnecessary and undesirable complication in improving the space available at Westlake Avenue.

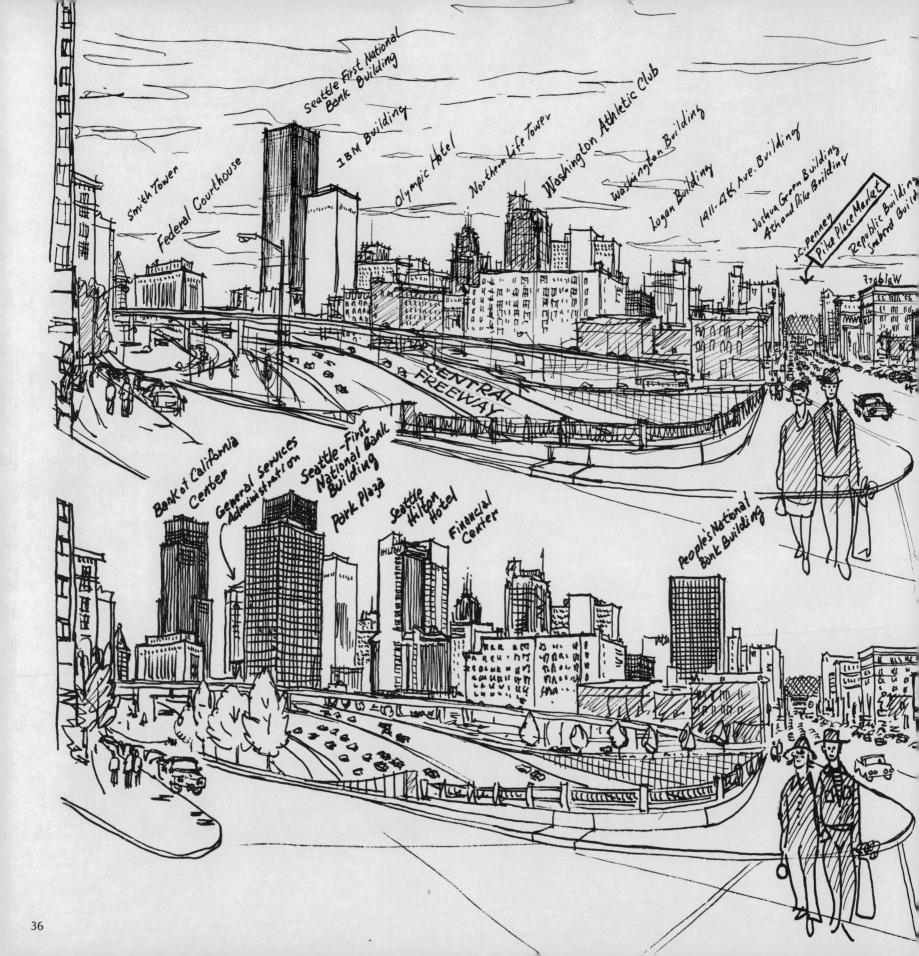

Smith Tower

Federal Courthouse

Seattle First National Bank Building

IBM Building

Olympic Hotel

Northern Life Tower

Washington Athletic Club

Washington Building

Logan Building

1411-4th Ave. Building

Joshua Green Building 4th and Pike Building

J.C. Penney

Pike Place Market

Republic Building
Seaboard Building

CENTRAL FREEWAY

Bank of California Center

General Services Administration

Seattle-First National Bank Building

Park Plaza

Seattle Hilton Hotel

Financial Center

People's National Bank Building

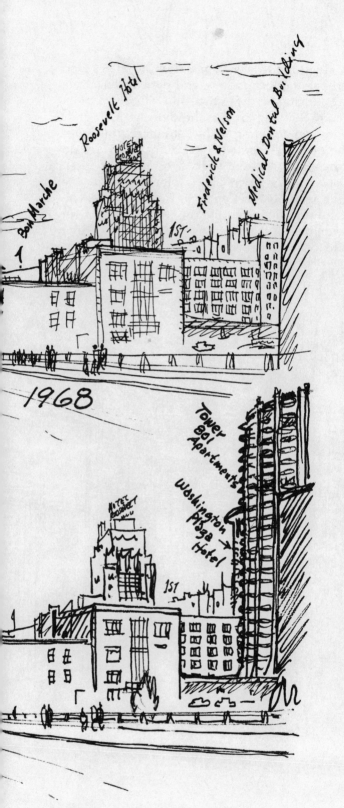

Bon Marche

Roosevelt Hotel

Frederick & Nelson

Medical-Dental Building

HOTEL ROOSEVELT

1ST

1968

Tower 801 Apartments

Washington Plaza Hotel

HOTEL ROOSEVELT

1ST

1973

These two views from Pike Street and Terry Avenue, although sketched only five years apart in 1968 and 1973, show the physical progress of the central business district development as downtown becomes more fertile for high-rise development. The commercial real-estate exploitation greatly needs to be matched by residential accommodation so that downtown does not become solely a daytime city. There must be the kind of attraction that can come only from people living there. The location of the great ditch barrier of the Central Freeway has cut downtown off from its natural nearby residential community on First Hill, thwarting the growth of that area in the process. The question posed by these two views is whether or not Seattle is a better place in which to live and work as a result of the developments and structures that have so markedly changed its skyline.

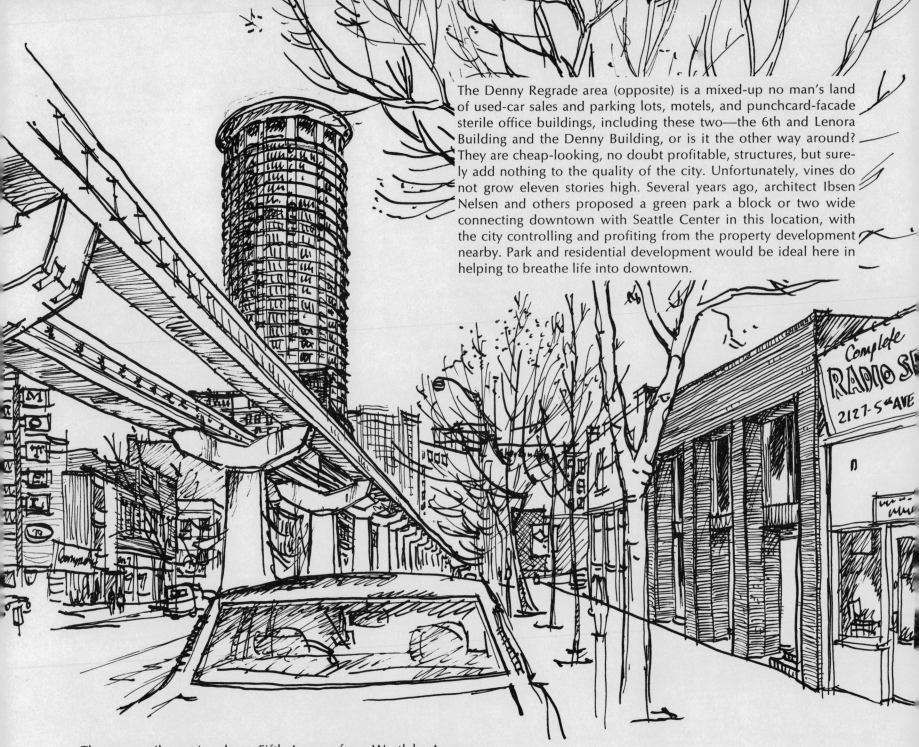

The Denny Regrade area (opposite) is a mixed-up no man's land of used-car sales and parking lots, motels, and punchcard-facade sterile office buildings, including these two—the 6th and Lenora Building and the Denny Building, or is it the other way around? They are cheap-looking, no doubt profitable, structures, but surely add nothing to the quality of the city. Unfortunately, vines do not grow eleven stories high. Several years ago, architect Ibsen Nelsen and others proposed a green park a block or two wide connecting downtown with Seattle Center in this location, with the city controlling and profiting from the property development nearby. Park and residential development would be ideal here in helping to breathe life into downtown.

The monorail, running down Fifth Avenue from Westlake Avenue and Pine Street through the Denny Regrade to the Seattle Center, is an unrealistic remnant of the Century 21 exposition of 1962. The mile run is too short for the trains to get up to full speed; nevertheless, the monorail continues on as a kind of tourists' toy, preventing tree-lined Fifth Avenue from fulfilling its destiny as a proper boulevard.

39

The Pike Place Market has had many trials and tribulations during the last twenty years, and yet it is doing very well. Not the least of its problems has been the long-time threat of large-scale demolition and drastic change through urban renewal, while the negligence of property owners and the avarice of would-be developers and their political cohorts have also contributed to the adverse circumstances. Seattle citizens, however, led by a group called the Friends of the Market, have shown that they valued the market by voting overwhelmingly for an initiative ordinance to protect and help continue it through the establishment of a seven-acre historical district. Even though the stated purpose of urban renewal is to save the market, urban renewal plans and activities present serious difficulties and threats to survival that require continuing vigilance by concerned citizens. The survival of the low-cost market and its neighborhood appears to depend ultimately upon public control and subsidy of essential market uses and properties.

The market is an outstanding and unique part of the Seattle scene. It offers an urban educational experience that enables people, and especially children, to see facets of humanity, activities, and aspects of the city not easily accessible elsewhere. Because there is no better place to shop for the best fresh produce, for out-of-the-ordinary foods, and for inexpensive goods of all kinds, the market is a prime shopping area for low-income people as well as for gourmets of every economic level. Nowhere else is there to be found such a broad social mixture going about its business in a natural and uninhibited way. People of all races, all religions, all nationalities, and all income levels come together freely to work and shop, to linger and look and enjoy themselves in an easy atmosphere traditionally and necessarily free of prejudice. Here is the dramatic experience of people acting out their daily existence through face-to-face encounter and involvement, in contrast to the sterile, dehumanizing environment that has grown to be typical of much of our urban world.

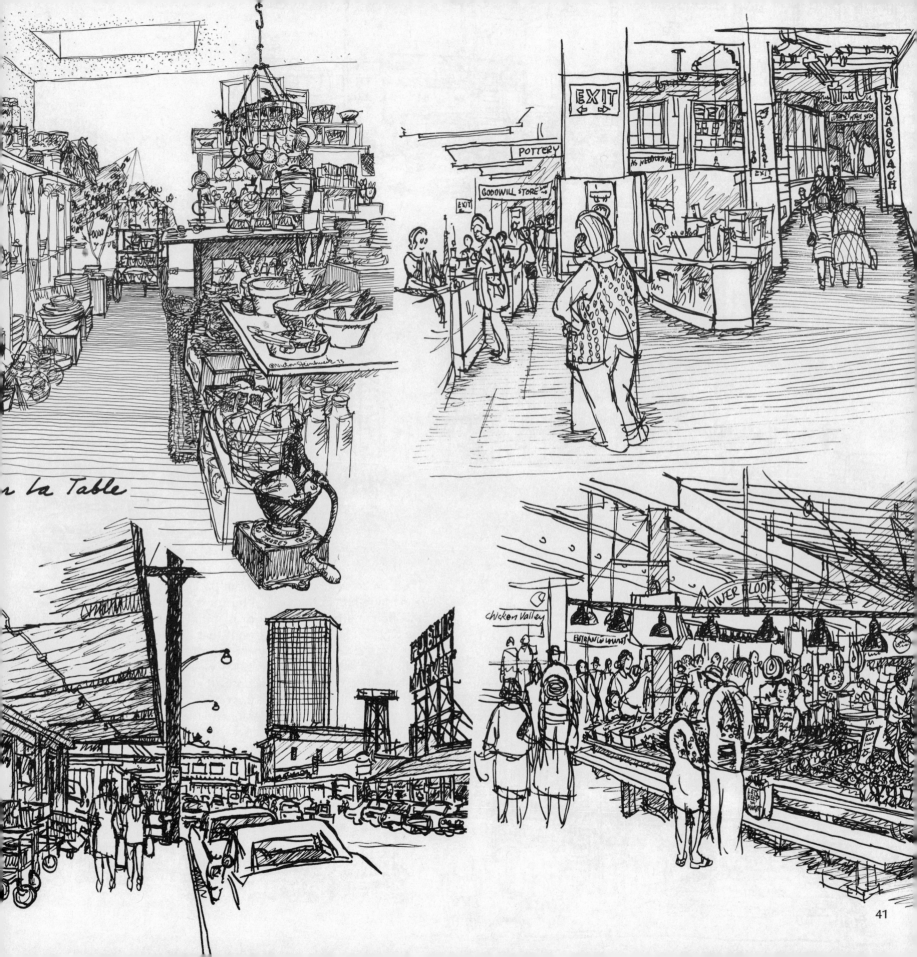

EXIT

POTTERY

GOODWILL STORE

EXIT

SASQUACH

La Table

PUBLIC MARKET

chicken Valley

LOWER FLOOR

ENTRANCE

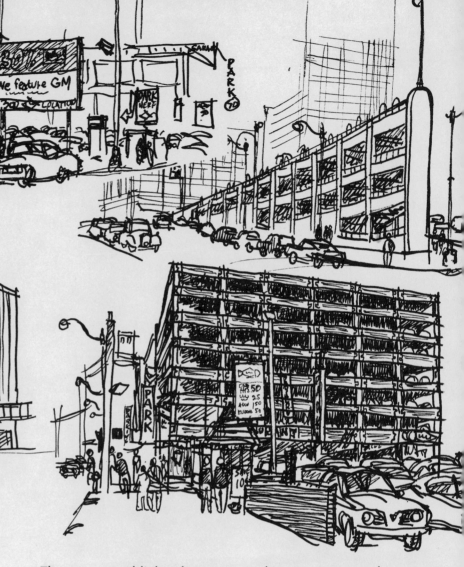

The cancerous blight of concrete parking structures and vast seas of parking lots in the central business district, where once livable and humane buildings stood, is rapidly destroying the fabric of the city. The justification given is that business must be served, as if it can be served only by the private automobile; yet, as each building is demolished to make way for a more tax-profitable asphalt area, downtown becomes that much less of an attraction and there is that much less to come to. Subsidized public transit is the only answer to the transportation need. Planning should begin for people-oriented uses of the parking lots as they are inevitably phased out in the future.

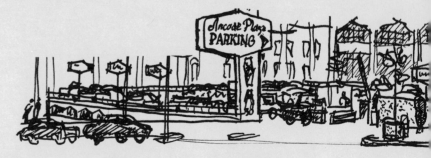

An older residential area west of Seattle Center has undergone considerable redevelopment in the last ten or fifteen years, with a plethora of small office structures of all shapes, sizes, and styles springing up—each as though none of the others existed. It is a zooland of modern Seattle architecture in a state of chaos, although many individual buildings are fairly well designed and have won architectural design awards. The Space Needle gives the clue to the proximity of Seattle Center.

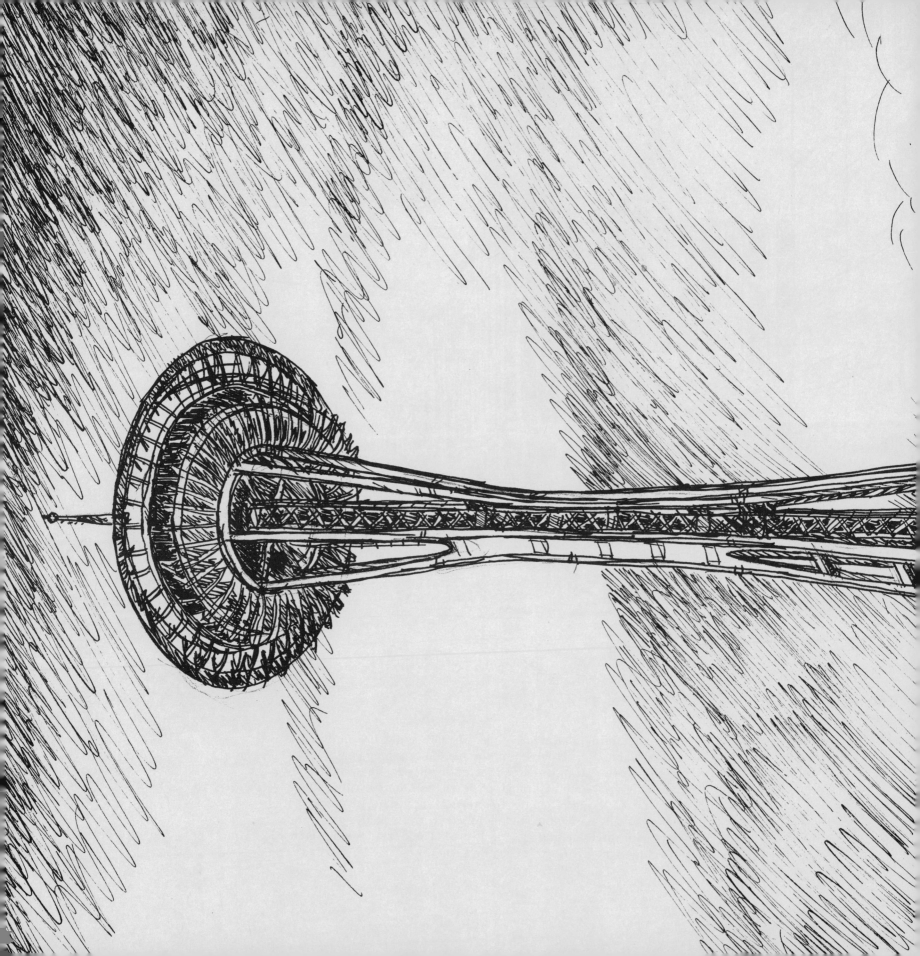

The symbol of Seattle's Century 21 exposition of 1962, now an established and familiar landmark, is the highly profitable, privately owned Space Needle, with its revolving restaurant at an elevation of five hundred feet. Its form, more sculptural than structurally expressive, is derived from designs in 1961 by Victor Steinbrueck, who was employed for that purpose by the principal firm of John Graham and Company, architects and engineers. The abstract white, mock-Gothic arches of the Pacific Science Center were designed for the Century 21 exposition by Detroit architect Minoru Yamasaki. In spite of their local prominence, neither structure has achieved architectural fame for design quality beyond the city limits of Seattle.

45

The Seattle Center International Fountain, with its changing water display and coordinated music, is the result of an international competition won by two young Japanese, Kazuyuki Matsushita and Hideki Shimizu, in 1959. It was brought to its present state of completion for the Century 21 exposition with landscaping ably developed by landscape architects Richard Haag Associates. They were also responsible for the excellent quality of the luxuriant planting, which does wonders to unify the miscellaneous architecture of the entire Seattle Center grounds.

One of the most pleasant and esthetically satisfying spaces in the Puget Sound area is the enclosed court of the Playhouse theater in Seattle Center. The magnificent bronze sculpture fountain by artist James H. FitzGerald graciously dominates the miscellaneous planting and high loggia. Suggestive of Pacific Northwest natural forms, the sculpture transcends realism and is as close to a masterpiece as any work in this area. Kirk, Wallace, McKinley and Associates were the architects of the buildings and the connecting loggia.

This authentic Northwest Indian ceremonial house in the Pacific Science Center is a museum of Indian artifacts. The building is a reconstruction of the house of Chief John Scow, built at the turn of the century on Gilford Island in British Columbia. The house poles are restored, and the front is a copy of the original Kwakiutl design. Anthropologist and Indian expert Bill Holm was in charge of the project. Appreciation for the cultural and ethnic quality of such work is deservedly increasing.

Another excellent example of a longhouse front is Ivar's Salmon House on the north shore of Lake Union. It is one of very few realistic and authentic Indian designs used commercially. Steve Brown and Tom Spear did the painting, and the totem poles were carved by Bill Neidinger for Ivar. There is additional good Indian art in the interior by Indian carver Duane Pasco. The natural landscaping helps to give the illusion of the real thing if the observer closes his ears and looks only straight ahead.

At Fourteenth Avenue South and South Jackson Street there is a fantastic display of visual pollution by public and private enterprise. The overhead wires and utility poles have been reduced a little in the last decade. The poles are shorter, and there are fewer crossbars, but a galaxy of forms still assails the eye. In the past, environmentalists were led to believe that the city would take realistic steps to eliminate such offenses, but time has shown that neither the general public nor its elected and appointed officials has the necessary understanding and concern. It is still to be hoped that increased awareness will eventually bring about correction of these civic outrages.

Streets that ought to be boulevards and were apparently originally so intended, such as Rainier Avenue South (above) and Aurora Avenue (below), while affording glimpses of scenic splendors, are all the more outrageous, as eyesores typical of less glamorously endowed American cities, because they violate Seattle's very nature as a place of amenity.

Angling to the northeast, East Madison Street from Twenty-third Avenue East offers a panorama of a pleasant single-family residential hillside with Lake Washington beyond. From a distance there appears to be a remarkable abundance of foliage, but this is not so apparent at the street level. Madison Street was once a boulevard, with trees lining both sides, linking the downtown area with the ferryboat landing at Lake Washington. Widening of the pavement to accommodate automobile traffic eliminated the trees and started the deterioration of the street.

51

Typical of this city of hills, this view from Thirty-first Avenue East and East Pine Street, first drawn in 1961, has remained relatively unchanged. It still shows the characteristic single-family homes on rolling, hilly topography, with much greenery punctuated by utility poles. In the middle distance is the luxuriant verdure of the University of Washington Arboretum, which contributes to both visual and recreational enjoyment. Beyond are the University of Washington and the University district. Even at this distance, the high-rise tower of Safeco Insurance looms objectionably above the skyline of university buildings, as forms and textures fade into space and sky. The many rolling hills of Seattle, which allow considerable visibility of known locations and landmarks, give a sense of security and confidence to persons moving about, as well as a great awareness of sky and clouds as a daily experience.

The West Seattle Freeway is a good place from which to see the downtown skyline while traveling at forty miles per hour. The view is even better at night. Here most of the familiar old and new landmarks are visible. From left to right these are: the three Queen Anne Hill television towers, the Seattle Center Coliseum, the Space Needle, the very distant Safeco Insurance tower in the University district, the General Services Administration Building, the Sea-First Building, the Bank of California Center, and the old Smith Tower—in all their vertical glory. In the middle distance are Elliott Bay and Harbor Island, with its marine and industrial activity. The freeways have made the city more visible. Perhaps this will bring about increased appreciation of its truly wonderful setting, which should, in turn, lead to a greater emphasis on environmental protection and enhancement.

SPEED
LIMIT
40

53

The "Counterbalance" of Queen Anne Avenue North drops rapidly into Elliott Bay, opening up a distant floating world where space, sky, mountains, and water are a continual source of surprise and delight. This vista and panorama are familiar to all Seattleites. The Counterbalance was named for the old streetcar system of cables under the street, which were hooked onto the cars to make the steep ascent possible and the descent safe. Views such as this, which are almost commonplace in Seattle, give an impression of overall scenic beauty that has not been fulfilled by city planning or by the quality of actual buildings. It is as though these things did not matter; one can always look away beyond to the distant amenities.

The Lake Washington Ship Canal (opposite) was dug in 1917 to connect Lake Washington, Lake Union, and Puget Sound as an aid in the commercial development of the inland waters. It still serves this purpose, though it is used heavily by pleasure boats passing to and from Puget Sound and its vast saltwater cruising world. Fringed with commercial establishments, the waterway defines the edges of Queen Anne, Magnolia, Ballard, and Fremont districts. Several years ago, as the result of public-spirited citizen efforts, both sides of the canal were lined with trees. The nearby Fremont Bridge has been painted a bright signal orange as a result of local community action, thereby effectively and literally adding color to the scene.

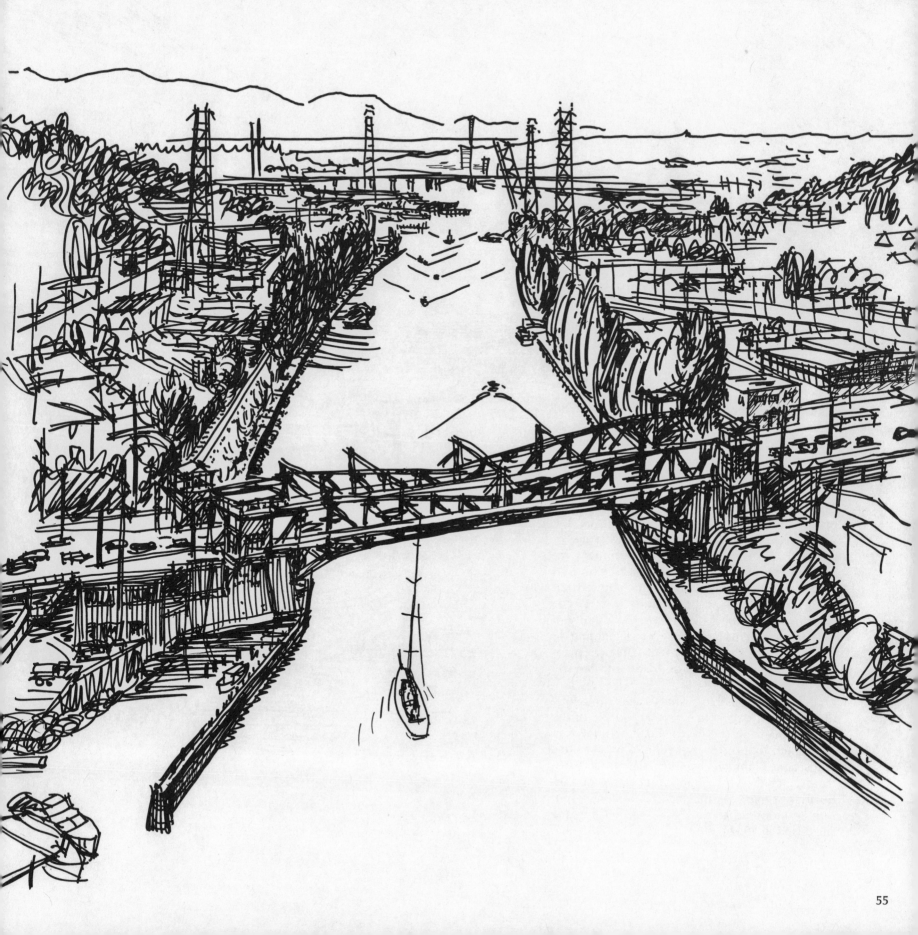

Lake Union has been the site of planning and zoning controversies for years, while private exploitation has continued along with the improvement of a few street ends for public use. This landlocked body of water should be regarded as a potentially excellent public amenity to be fittingly developed for the enhancement of its surroundings and the benefit of the whole city. Instead, it has been the scene of rampant real-estate speculation, with many inappropriate and offensive projects along its shores and over its waters. Public-spirited citizens, led by those in the floating homes who are close enough, recognize the incongruity of the developments and have been fighting to make the lake a civic asset with effective planning which still needs to be made into law.

One of the good things that is actually taking place is the creation of a park at the site of the old gas plant on the north shore, as shown in the sketch (opposite) by Laurie Olin. Sensitive landscape planning by Richard Haag Associates, including the retention of interesting industrial artifacts, is making this strategic spot into a unique urban park—as *Seattle Cityscape* suggested in 1962.

Along the shores of Lake Union and Portage Bay, people have been happily living in floating homes, of obviously anonymous and often low-cost design, for many years. As available spaces have decreased, moorage costs have risen excessively, and the whole bohemian houseboat way of life is threatened.

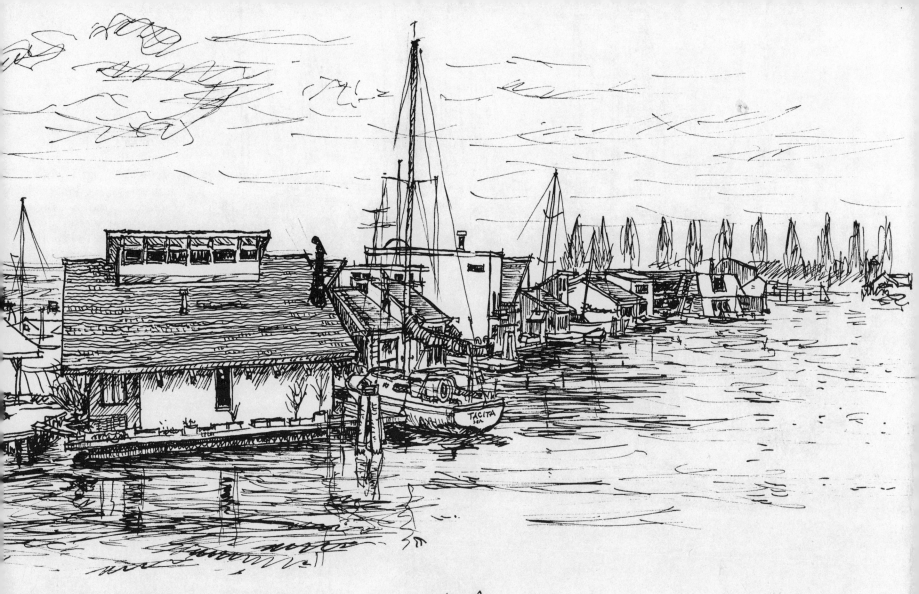

It would be unfortunate if this colorful style of living were lost to the city, even though a new, expensive breed of quality-designed luxurious contemporary houseboats is beginning to appear, especially in Portage Bay. Their posh life style is attractive, too, but for a more affluent sector.

Fisherman's Wharf near the Ballard Bridge is a real working boat area where hundreds of commercial fishermen moor their boats and work on their equipment. There is nothing phony or artificial here.

The Hiram M. Chittenden Locks make it possible to raise and lower vessels that pass between saltwater Puget Sound and the fresh waters of Lake Union and Lake Washington. Boats of all sizes and their crews, on their way to and from the many sailing and fishing locations, present a view of a kind of Seattle life difficult to match anywhere in the world.

Shilshole breakwater and boat harbor, just off the Puget Sound entrance to Lake Washington Ship Canal, are a joy to sailors and landlubbers alike. Records show more than 225,000 pleasure boats in the Puget Sound area, and the enlarged Shilshole Bay Marina is a recognition of the economic importance of boating, as well as its amenity value for the city. Water is a vital part of the city, surrounding and embracing it, while serving as a great visual and recreational asset. The Port of Seattle owns and operates this facility.

The United States Navy piers at Smith's Cove have been phased out and consequently are the subject of intense controversy regarding their future. The Port of Seattle hopes to utilize this location for container ship operations, while local residents are anxious to have it put to a use more compatible with the adjoining Queen Anne and Magnolia residential communities. The monumental Port of Seattle grain elevators, built before the eyes of unsuspecting home owners in recent years, have alerted them to take action to avoid future noxious environmental disturbances. In another location, the grain elevators could have been an exciting industrial landmark.

The massive and ungainly Lake Washington Ship Canal freeway bridge over the northeastern tip of Lake Union looms ponderously over Eastlake Avenue East as the University district is approached from the south. There are many beautiful bridges in the world; one like this, however, can only suggest a lost opportunity to contribute to the quality of the cityscape. The recently completed Safeco Insurance Building has become another objectionable high-rise landmark, visible for miles around. In an otherwise pleasantly scaled community it serves as a monument to excessive and inappropriate land use, bringing nothing to the neighborhood except a violation of the pedestrian scale of the street, and additional traffic congestion. It is a competently designed structure, but it belongs elsewhere—not on the skyline or in the community of the University district.

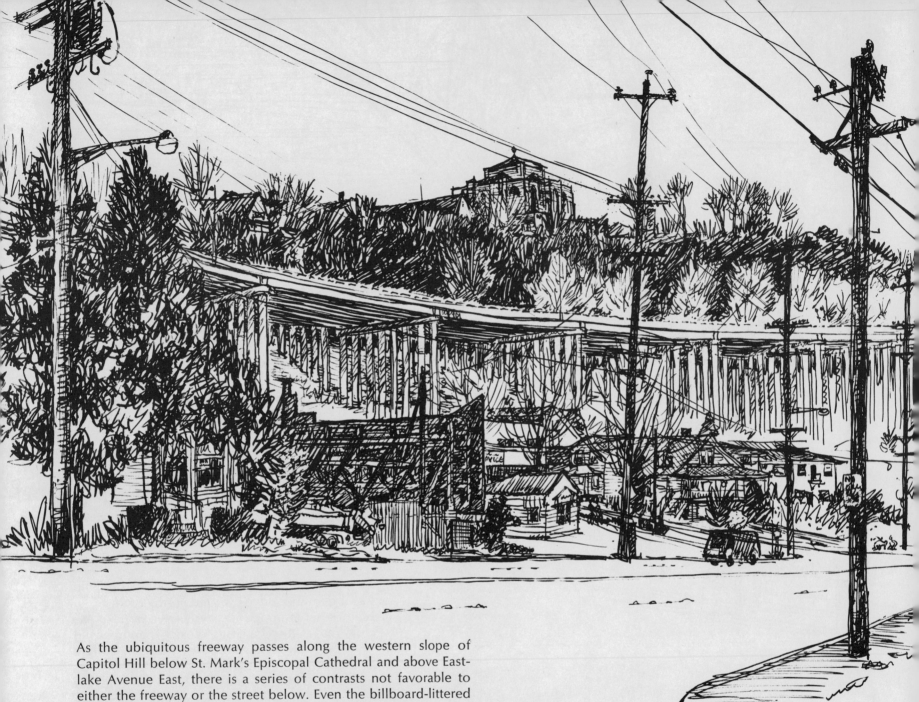

As the ubiquitous freeway passes along the western slope of Capitol Hill below St. Mark's Episcopal Cathedral and above East-lake Avenue East, there is a series of contrasts not favorable to either the freeway or the street below. Even the billboard-littered street is not so objectionable as the overmonumental, land-destroying, noise-producing, air-polluting concrete monstrosity so prominently located and displayed against the green wooded hillside. Chaotic and incongruous scenes like this one are far too typical as freeways have autocratically moved through the city.

This honest, functional counterweight bridge, located in the industrial area along West Waterway at Spokane Street, contributes an interesting dramatic element in the cityscape. It is one of many bridges over the city's waterways which give character and interest. Some bridges have been neglected and allowed to deteriorate, and it is surely to be desired that the rebuilding program will provide for future designs of high esthetic quality.

65

The Port of Seattle's busy container ship accommodation has changed the face of the working waterfront. Most land and sea cargo is now handled in freightcar-size metal containers by huge cranes. Extensive open storage areas are required, as here along the East Waterway.

Ships move in and out much more rapidly, and individual handling of cargos by longshoremen is becoming a thing of the past. Brightly colored and dramatically lighted at night, the port's massive cranes bring excitement and interest to the water's edge. Ships and the sea have always been close to Seattle's heart and part of its lore.

Shipping and related commerce are also a significant part of the economic basis of the Puget Sound region, although there is now relatively little passenger service except to Alaska. The Port of Seattle has been responsible for many changes in the appearance as well as the functioning of the city. Within their own realm these have usually been well planned and designed, but there has been minimal coordination of the port projects with overall city planning. It is generally recognized that effective city planning has not existed in Seattle for many years.

For too long the Boeing Company has been the most important economic base of Seattle. The Boeing industrial empire in this area ranges at least from Auburn, just south of the city, north to Mukilteo, and its effects are felt throughout the Pacific Northwest, even as its planes fly throughout the world. The region's dependency on the health of this single industry has been crippling at times, while at other times it has resulted in a deceptive prosperity. The many overwhelmingly large plant structures fronted by rows of gigantic aircraft are physical testimony to the size of the industry and have destroyed the Green River Valley for farming. Boeing's part in Seattle's economy and expansion since World War II has been large; its contribution to cultural and social quality has been negligible.

Along East Marginal Way South there are many heavy industries served by rail and by the adjacent Duwamish waterway. Dramatic factory shapes are becoming even more spectacular as air pollution prevention measures require additional structures such as this huge, clawlike top to the Northwestern Glass Company building. Most of the industrial plant grounds are not accessible to the public; they are, however, a vivid part of the cityscape with their functionally engineered forms. Landscaping attempts are usually vain, token gestures directed toward the proponents of a "city beautiful."

The University of Washington has acquired a new image with the completion of several new buildings enclosing a plaza in front of Suzzallo Library, where grass and footpaths previously existed. The red brick plaza covers a 1,200-car parking garage, exhaust-vented through the three shafted "campaniles" which have become symbolically and visually the crown of the campus. The plaza, reminiscent of the Piazza del Campo in Siena, Italy, sorely needs humanizing to relieve its empty severity. The rugged Kane Hall facade, while capably designed, is brutal and ponderous, unlike the more pleasantly scaled, older, eclectic "collegiate Gothic" buildings that flank Rainier Vista, as seen on the following page.

Architecture Hall

Balmer Hall

Sieg Hall

Guthrie Hall

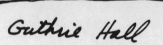

Loew Hall

Along with the predominant eclectic style of "collegiate Gothic" architecture on the University of Washington campus, there are some older buildings that are well maintained, such as the handsome Architecture Hall, in Renaissance Revival style, built at the time of the 1909 Alaska-Yukon Pacific exposition from the design of architect John Galen Howard. The severity and lack of refinement of many of the otherwise competent new buildings make the older buildings more to be admired and cherished.

In spite of some architectural inadequacies, the campus is a pleasant city within the city, and it is obvious that much care has been taken to keep it so.

Aerospace Research Laboratory

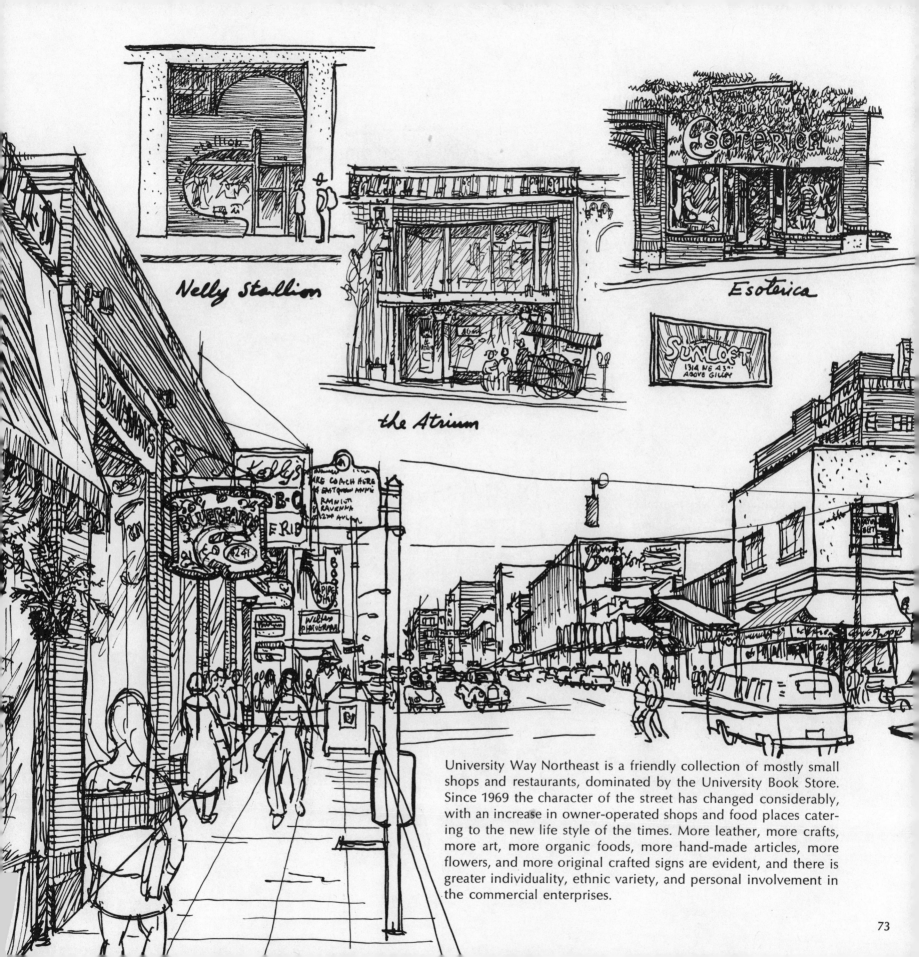

Nelly Stallion

Esoterica

the Atrium

University Way Northeast is a friendly collection of mostly small shops and restaurants, dominated by the University Book Store. Since 1969 the character of the street has changed considerably, with an increase in owner-operated shops and food places catering to the new life style of the times. More leather, more crafts, more art, more organic foods, more hand-made articles, more flowers, and more original crafted signs are evident, and there is greater individuality, ethnic variety, and personal involvement in the commercial enterprises.

A valiant attempt has been made to rescue University Way from the automobile and give it to people on foot, thereby increasing its livability, attractiveness, and economic viability. In 1955 Victor Steinbrueck proposed redevelopment of the street as a shopper's mall. The concept was further studied and developed by Richardson Associates in 1972 in extensive collaboration with community interests.

These sketches by Bill Isley for Richardson Associates suggest some of the interesting possibilities of their proposals, which unfortunately were not accepted by the majority of the property owners. The deleterious conflict with the motor car continues, however, and it is reasonable to expect that some such intelligent planning will eventually prevail.

The shopping center of West Seattle is here along California Avenue Southwest near Southwest Alaska Street. While there are a few larger chain stores, it is mainly composed of small and varied shops catering to the largely white, middle-class population. West Seattle is almost surrounded by salt water, but its involvement with the water seems to be mainly recreational. It is a district of well-kept, single-family homes somewhat smugly isolated from the rest of the city.

Northwest Market Street is the shopping axis of Ballard, a typical city neighborhood that nevertheless retains its own unique character. Once a separate town, Ballard still has some of that quality, with its own local branches of some of the large chain stores. Its special accent and flavor come from the large percentage of persons of Scandinavian descent living there, and from work and activities related to the nearby waterway and bay. The plethora of drive-in establishments of all sorts a few blocks to the east at Fifteenth Northwest is an unfortunate commercial mess which makes this older pedestrian street more attractive.

Fremont is one of the early towns that became part of the city. It had long passed its heyday and was relatively dormant until, in recent years, it was discovered by people with a new life style. Now activity and vitality have come to this district, with creative, young, free-living people taking advantage of cheap rents for the old buildings. Long hair, beards, colorful ancient or hand-crafted garments, communal living, and friendliness seem to be the symbols and expressions of their mode of life. At any rate, they have brought action to the old place.

Bellevue, while not within Seattle's boundaries, is part of the metropolitan area. It is identified as a "bedroom community," most of whose residents commute to work in the city. Since it has grown up for and by the automobile, pedestrians are an anomaly; it is easier to drive around the shopping district than to walk. Bellevue has just recently been incorporated into the metropolitan transit system, however, so it is to be hoped that dependence on the private automobile will decrease there as elsewhere.

When one looks at the city as a whole, the series of patterns of building masses, trees, and yards are conceivable as textures. The north slope of Queen Anne Hill seen from Aurora Avenue North presents the "urban texture" of Seattle in a most obvious and typical fashion. This texture is composed of gable- and hip-roofed middle-class houses, usually on grades a little above the street, with uniform yards and an abundant scattering of trees, and with the omnipresent thorns of utility poles crisscrossing to the skyline, which in this view is punctuated only by house, tree, and pole. Color is important, adding to richness of the scene.

A tidy, well-kept street of miscellaneous small homes in Ballard along Northwest Sixty-second Street could be almost anywhere in Seattle, although there are differences. The scattering of wooden house styles over such a long period is less typical of the city since this is one of the oldest neighborhoods. Most houses have been "modernized" several times, and this has tended to homogenize the styles. Victorian details are removed, roof overhangs are cropped, cedar sidewalls are covered with aluminum siding or imitation brick or stone, wood sashes are replaced with aluminum, and wrought-iron railings are substituted for wooden ones. A contemporary house of the 1960s has been added to the group. Consequently the neighborhood is a sort of stylistic architectural "melting pot" and yet is quite characteristic of Seattle.

Thirty-sixth Avenue East near East Madison Street in the Washington Park neighborhood is a lovely tree-lined street of large family homes. It has always been a "prestige" neighborhood and seems likely to remain so. Most of the homes were designed for prosperous families by well-known Seattle architects in the first quarter of the century. Although the homes are pleasant and well designed, with generous yards, the stately street trees are largely responsible for the quality of the street. There has been much political talk of street tree planting in the last decade, but more trees have been cut down than have been planted. The street tree-planting programs have never got into the ground, except in a very few situations where diligent citizen involvement has prevailed over City Hall reluctance.

79

1960's

1920's

1910's

The marks of their eras are on many streets as their residential style identifies the decade in which they were built. Except for the early years, the house styles appear to fit neatly into each calendar decade, forming a visual history of the growth of the city. The character of their times is also expressed in the homes themselves, suggesting that a similar lesson could be learned from what is built today. Individual homes are often overlaid with "improvements" or "modernizations" that are unfavorably revealing of changing occupancy.

When the Seattle Freeway (opposite) gouged its way along the western slope of Capitol Hill in the early 1960s, it exposed a clear panoramic view from the properties above, which were quickly built upon to capitalize on this asset so cherished in Seattle. The broad view is surely marvelous; however, it unfortunately includes eight or ten lanes of busy concrete highway with the ensuing noise and air pollution as a disturbing environmental negative. The architecture of the various apartments is neither generally harmonious nor of high quality, but these do form an interesting, variegated, architectural wall above the roadways. Another negative factor of the freeway is the fact that it serves as a barrier to east-west traffic, since there are few crossings.

Most Seattleites do not realize that probably close to 4 percent of the population lives in mobile home parks such as this one at Northeast Eighty-fifth Street and Lake City Way Northeast. Although the county and city have imposed restrictive controls on mobile homes and their locations, they continue to increase because they satisfy a need for an economical home. Many are indeed economical, but there are some very luxurious mobile homes as well. Basic physical needs are compactly provided by the units, and yet the total environment seems to be substandard and an unsatisfactory substitute for a permanent home.

A different type of home is cropping up in the suburbs, as illustrated by this "planned unit" development east of Bellevue. Zoning laws allow planning to differ from the ordinary single-family platted residential lots when a larger group area is designed. There can be advantages both for the resident and for the developer. While some units are rented, many are sold as condominiums. According to the advertisements, this is the "young executive" way of life.

The family of architect Peter Staten lives in this generous, comfortable family home on Capitol Hill near Volunteer Park. It is of a nameless style common in the first decade of this century and prevalent in areas of Capitol Hill, Mount Baker Park, Queen Anne, Madrona, and the University districts, which were developed at that time. The garage was undoubtedly added later, along with the iron railings on the porch roof.

It is not surprising that many capable contemporary architects and others have found value in older houses in established neigh-borhoods. The neighborhoods usually have all necessary improvements, including sidewalks, and are convenient to schools, shopping, and sometimes even parks. Landscaping is often complete and well grown. The houses provide space economically, with larger rooms and higher ceilings than are common in new houses. If he wishes, the architect may use his design talents to work within the existing form to achieve a more contemporary functional interior layout.

1860's

1870's

1880's

1900's

1910's

1920's

1930's

1940's

1950's

1960's

1970's

84

1890's

Seattle's residential history is visible in the changing house styles through the years since its pioneering beginning in the middle of the last century. The stages of neighborhood growth show in the recognizable house styles of the houses. These sketches are of middle-class homes characteristic of each decade. Of course other styles occurred in each period.

One of the most picturesque styles, which has become even more precious because it cannot now be duplicated, or hardly even restored, is the Victorian style of the 1890s, illustrated by these two beautiful but neglected small houses at East John Street near Twenty-second Avenue East. They are stock-built, similar, but interestingly different in carpenter details. Seattle has seemed almost ashamed of its architectural heritage until the present time, when it is too late for many significant landmarks which have been lost.

There are still dairy and produce farms in the Green River Valley in spite of the intrusion of industry, led by the Boeing Company, and the commercialization of the Southcenter shopping complex. It is a strange system of planning values that allows irreplaceable fertile topsoil to be covered with asphalt and concrete. Remaining farms are struggling for survival under the excess burden of unrealistic real-estate speculation and inflated property taxes. And much good farm land lies fallow, awaiting some fabulous price while the farmers have moved off the land.

Southcenter (opposite) is a lucrative commercialization of the propitious situation provided by the juncture of the various freeways, with most of the city's important retail enterprises prosperously involved while they issue complaints about the decrease of business in downtown Seattle. Parking is generously provided, and public transportation hardly exists. Except for the surrounding sea of parking, the shopping center concept is simply a plush modern version of the old village shopping street. It is completely dependent on the motor car.

Boeing Aerospace Center

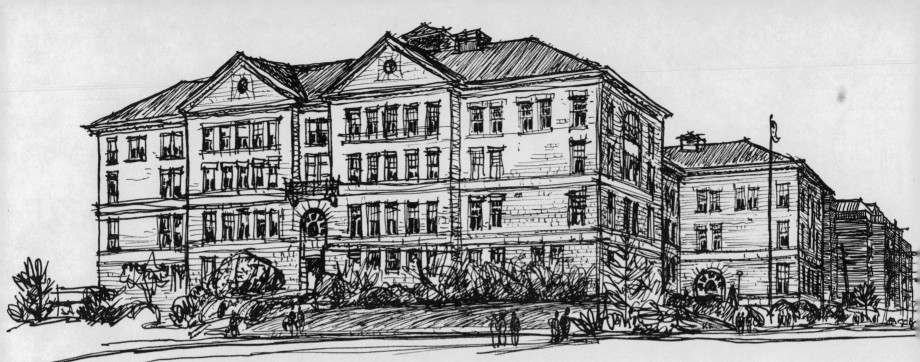

If there is an architectural landmark in the city, it must surely be old Broadway High School, built in 1902 and now a part of Central Seattle Community College. Its massive stone form has been witness to the education of generations of students, as well as a prominent element in the city scene. The potential for rehabilitation is excellent, both architecturally and economically. In an unassuming way, it is a handsome building in its own right, although derivative from Italian Renaissance Palace style. As part of the facility of the community college, it has been overcrowded and misused for several years, with the result that these faults have become associated with the quality of the building. Now it is doomed because unsympathetic architects and school authorities wish to build a megastructural monument, several blocks long, in the New Brutalism style of the red brick facility (below) crawling along Broadway toward the old building. The severity of their work has made the old building look even better. Hope prevails that preservation forces and economy may yet save Old Broadway for rehabilitation as an excellent classroom facility.

Persistent preservation efforts have saved the old Ballard Fire Station of 1908. It was threatened and almost lost as a result of the anxiety of Fire Department officials to replace it with a contemporary facility that would more efficiently meet their present needs. Citizens forced a public vote in 1972, and the picturesque building has been saved for other community uses.

Fire Station #34 in the Madison district is an interesting contemporary structure designed by architects Hobbs, Fukui Associates under the Forward Thrust program. It still looks like a fire station, while combining unusual geometric contemporary forms.

Still one of the finest churches in the Northwest is St. Joseph's Catholic Church, built in 1932. It is an exposed concrete structure, remarkable for that time, designed by architect Joseph Wilson of A. H. Albertson and Associates and built in the place of a more costly traditional building, which was begun, but fortunately had to be discarded because of the economic depression. It is architecture of enduring quality through the genius of its designer.

Two recent churches of excellent quality are St. Peter's Episcopal Church by architects Grant, Copeland, and Chervenak, and St. Demetrios Greek Orthodox Church by architect Paul Thiry.

The Isaac Ingalls Stevens School at 1242 Eighteenth Avenue East, built in 1902, makes an interesting contrast with the new Beacon Hill Elementary School of 1971 at 2025 Fourteenth Avenue South. The recent single-story school is well designed, pleasant, and safer, but lacks the visual stature, character, and interest of the older building. Architects were Durham, Anderson, Freed Company. Spice is added to the cityscape and to community life through retention of these old historical buildings in active use. Surely the quality of education is not adversely affected.

Examples of some of the better civic architectural projects built in the last decade are (from left to right) the Ballard Swimming Pool (architects Bindon and Wright), the Madrona Bathhouse–Dance Studio remodeling (Arne Bystrom), North Seattle Community College (Mahlum and Mahlum Architects), the Lake City Branch Library (John Morse and Associates), Fire Station #36 (Joyce, Copeland, Vaughan), and the Southwest Branch Library (Durham Anderson Freed Company). The range of fairly high quality civic design is illustrated, and these buildings do fit well into their locations. Some of these projects were built under the Forward Thrust capital improvement program, and the designs were reviewed as civic works by the Seattle Design Commission. The commission has been responsible for significant improvement in civic architecture in recent years.

Some of the most interesting of the Forward Thrust projects have been the small neighborhood "mini-parks" scattered throughout the city usually on vacant property. Some of the designs have been contrived and overworked, but the imaginative ones sketched are some of those which are well used and loved by the neighborhood children— the real test of quality. They are (from top down) the Leschi Playground (landscape architects Sakuma, James and Peterson), the Firehouse Mini Park (Richard Haag Associates), and Rainier Playfield (Bridges and Burke).

As in other cities, much of the layering over of buildings in recent years has been in the chain enterprise idiom. There is an impersonal, standard, plastic pattern to many of these commercial edifices which has tended to homogenize all of America. Banks with their many branches and parking lots are offenders as well. They cater to the motor car completely, thus carelessly destroying or at least mutilating and eroding the pedestrian streets as older buildings and smaller owner-operated enterprises are removed to make way for the new developments. Other, more personal, businesses, even though occasionally aggressive in appearance, may simply lend color and interest to the street. It seems to be a matter of personal involvement with the environment, or lack of it.

A tremendous modern transportation facility at Seattle-Tacoma International Airport has risen around the old terminal and runways. The Richardson Associates are the architects, engineers, and planners for the Port of Seattle, which owns and operates this vast concrete, steel, and glass complex. It appears to work efficiently as planned, although with some inevitable dehumanizing of participants in the process. The massiveness, the tremendous amount of space given over to the automobile, and the total physical complexity are too much for comfortable comprehension; and yet it is obviously a very successful project.

The parking garage is an incredible fantasy of spiral forms which suggest that it is some sort of monstrous grinder of automobiles and people.

The Seattle Freeway has result-ed in some remarkable visual effects beyond its purpose of providing an expeditious road-way for the automobile. Un-fulfilled hopes for the future by highway planners are ex-pressed in these curious un-finished elevated ramps to no-where in the vicinity of Con-necticut Street. They may yet become abstract monuments to the decline and fall of freeways in the interest of energy con-servation and pollution control.

Near South Spokane Street and Airport Way South the com-plexity of freeway traffic routes has created an unbelievably in-tricate intertwining of curving concrete ribbons leading to various somewheres from some-where else. From the ground this is a monumentally incred-ible roller coaster of abstract forms where landscaping can only be insignificant.

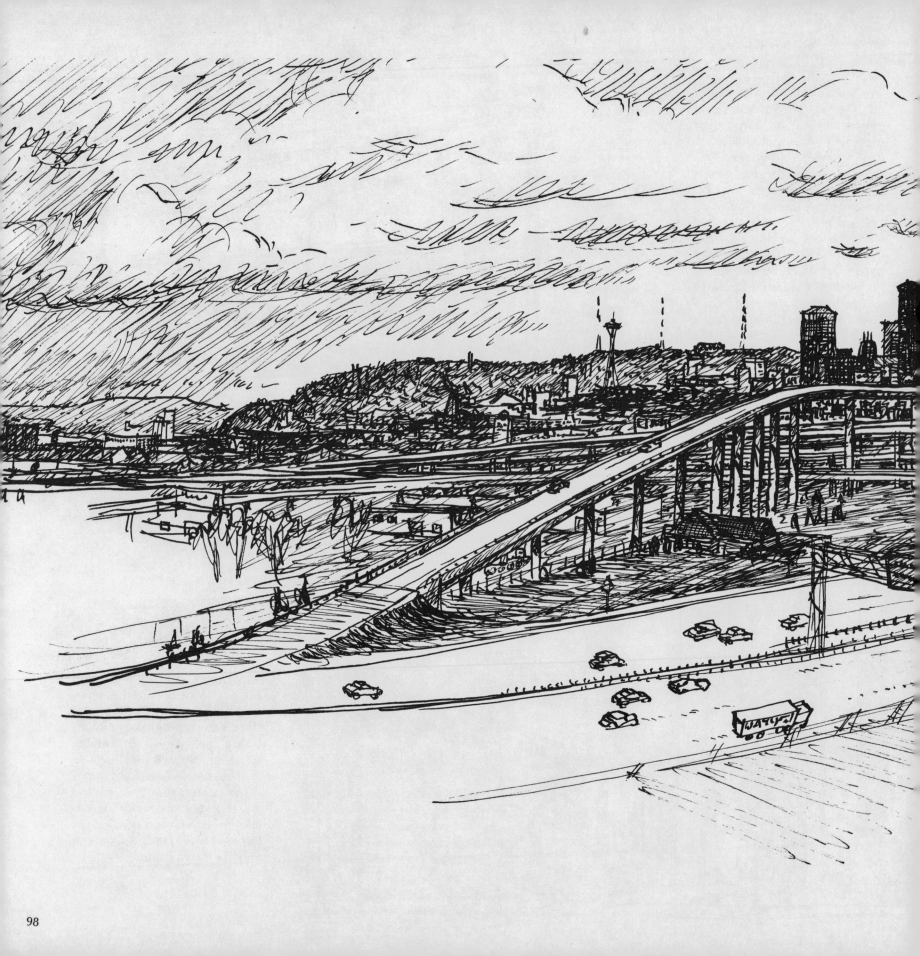

Approached from the south on the freeway, the central business district offers one of its best views, as the downtown buildings pile up together in a satisfying composition. The dominant structures of the highest high-rise buildings appear less overbearing when viewed in this linear relationship to one another. Most of the architectural landmarks can readily be identified since their owners and architects have sought to establish corporate identities through unique forms and details. The sweeping freeway structures nearby, however, make no concessions to any of them in size or visual dominance. In the past man's monuments were places of worship and governmental or civic buildings; now the real monuments of our time are freeways and high-rise commercial enterprises. The vision in motion experienced here is exciting and presents a dramatic, spectacular entrance to the city.

99

Under the leadership of Dr. Richard Fuller, now retired, the Seattle Art Museum grew to be the most important institution in the fine art activities of the city. Dr. Fuller and his mother, Mrs. Eugene Fuller, gave the building to the city. It was designed by architects Bebb and Gould and opened in 1933. The dignified white stone building is a refined example of the Art Deco and Beaux-Arts styles prevalent at that time. Isamu Noguchi was the sculptor of the *Black Sun,* one of the many public works of art that have recently begun to appear in the city.

Part of the boulevard system laid out by the Olmstead Brothers in the first decade of the century, Magnolia Boulevard remains an enduring pleasure with its colorful, twisting evergreen madrona trees offering a visual foil to the sweeping panorama of Elliott Bay and the hills and mountains beyond.

101

Fortunately there were influential, civic-minded visionaries in Seattle during the early days of this century. One of the really good things that took place as the result of their concern for the quality of the city was the layout and design of the boulevards which are almost continuous from Fort Lawton in the northwest section through the Magnolia, Interlaken, Montlake, Madrona, Leschi, and Rainier districts to Seward Park in the southeast. The routes are responsive to the topography and well landscaped with native trees and plants. They are planned to open to many lovely views

Magnolia Boulevard W. near W. Howe St.

Magnolia Boulevard W. from W. Montfort Place

Interlaken Boulevard E.

for the enjoyment and appreciation of characteristic topographic features of water and mountains. It is difficult to imagine Seattle without this fine boulevard system and even more difficult to imagine the present decision makers in the city providing such an altruistic amenity today. The sequential experience of a drive or cycle along these boulevards will always be enjoyed. The boulevards of 1905 set an example of civic improvement that must be matched in the future in other appropriate ways in order to make this the most livable city in America.

Mount Baker Beach

Lake Washington Boulevard & E. Huron St.

Lake Washington Boulevard E. & E. Harrison St.

A picturesque small foot bridge and aqueduct passes through the University of Washington Arboretum, fitting harmoniously into the natural setting. The simple structure of concrete and brick with its rhythmically spaced arches enhances the situation, providing an example of enduring architectural quality. Roads through the arboretum are held to a minimum as this plant and tree specimen park brings enjoyment to thousands, particularly from the central residential districts. Civic battles have been waged for years to keep expressways out and to retain the park for public enjoyment. Another controversy has been waged over possible fencing and continued university maintenance instead of the present general park use by the public, and the public appears to have lost to expediency.

Under the Forward Thrust program for improvement of Woodland Park Zoo, architect George Bartholick has planned a most remarkable and progressive revitalization into a humanitarian zoo for the benefit of both animals and animal lovers. The sensitively conceived proposal significantly increases the use of Woodland Park for people and as a relatively free-ranging home for animals in accord with present concerns for the care of wild species. Picnicking facilities will be increased considerably as well. The animal collection is to be exhibited in spaces which simulate their habitat and in which the animal is comfortable. Contact of the animals with people is minimized, while the opportunity for people to observe animals living naturally is maximized. A constructive and imaginative aspect of the proposal is to cover over a considerable length of Aurora Avenue with a conservatory building joining the two halves of the park severed by the highway in 1930.

Like saltwater Puget Sound on the west, freshwater Lake Washington provides powerful breathing space for Seattle at its eastern boundary. Beyond are the suburban "bedroom" towns of Kirkland, Houghton, Bellevue, Issaquah, Redmond, and Mercer Island, and the foothills of the Cascade Mountains. The extensive open panoramas of water, green hills, and mountains are a great visual amenity—perhaps deceptive as an illusory reminder of the nearness and availability of the wilderness wherein to escape the banalities and cruelties of the city.

Two floating concrete highway bridges are seen crossing the lake from separate viewpoints on north Capitol Hill at East Olin Place and from Thirtieth Avenue South near South Jackson Street. Forty years ago, ferryboats served the same purpose more pleasantly and even more expeditiously. More bridges are sought by highwaymen and fought by enlightened environmentalists. The automobile is increasing the use of the areas beyond the city, while inevitably making them less desirable in the very process. As the number of second homes for escaping city dwellers increases, they become part of the problem rather than the solution. Lake Washington is part of Seattle's natural superlativeness, but it is not indestructible, as many seem to believe.

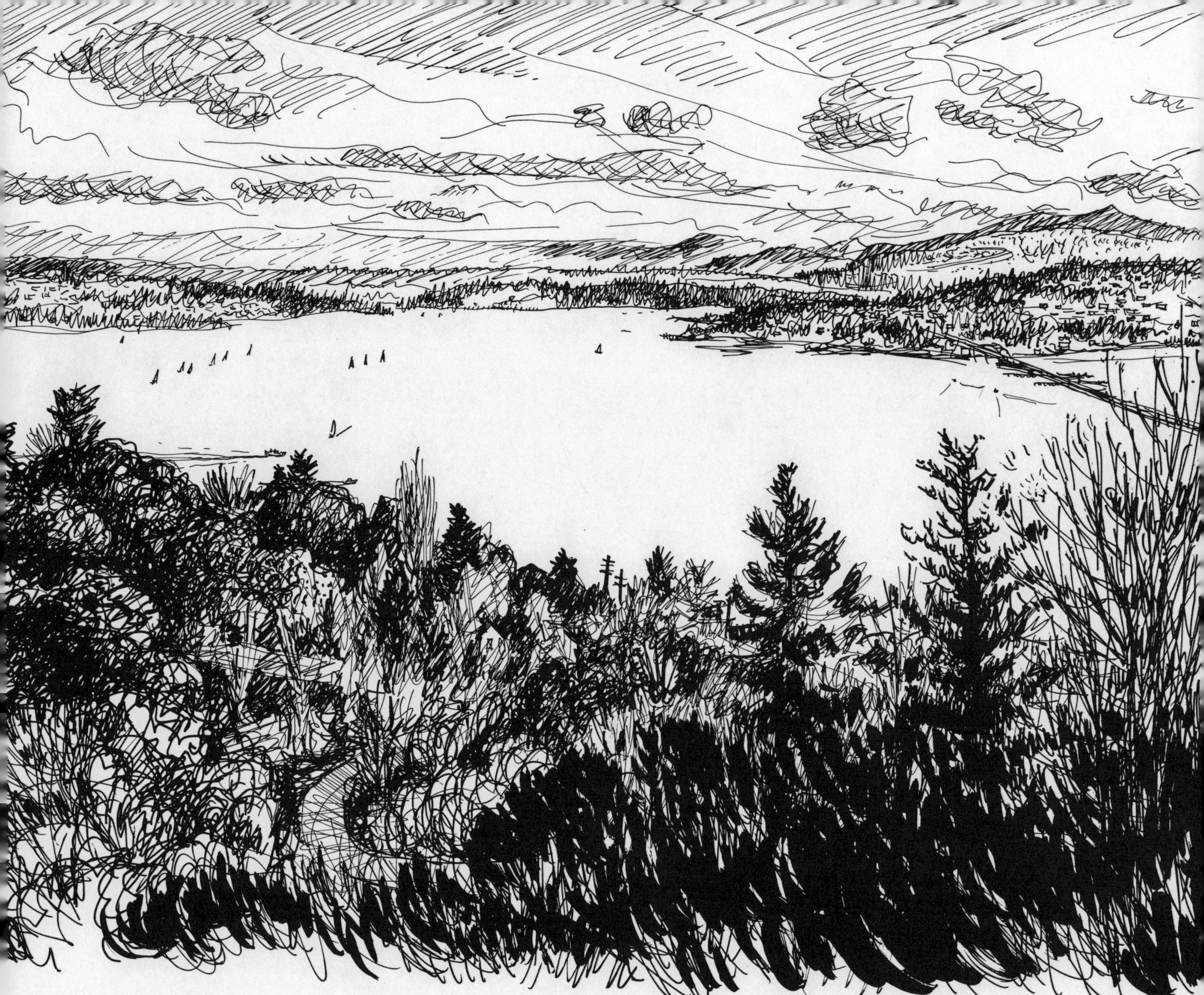

One of the most natural parks within the city is Seward Park, which has been logged off only once and is still relatively unspoiled and undeveloped. The large groves of twisted, colorful, evergreen madrona trees are a special Pacific Northwest phenomenon to be enjoyed along with the tall second-growth stands of Douglas fir and western red cedar. The park also abounds in undergrowth of salal, Oregon grape, and sword ferns. Picnic areas, beaches, and paths are in constant use in all seasons. There is also provision for outdoor concerts in a natural amphitheater. Careful and sensitive planning could improve the recreational potential of Seward Park by creatively increasing access and special use of more spaces.

Golden Gardens Park is a sandy, wind-swept, driftwood-strewn stretch of saltwater beach. Here one can beachcomb, stroll, or just sit on a log and look at the sea and the mountains. The air is definitely fresher here. For several years Golden Gardens was the subject of controversy as a possible location for an aquarium. The preservation of the beach as a more or less natural place finally won out, and the aquarium is to be located near the central waterfront. As a result of the dispute, citizens learned to care a little more for the quality of places that already exist. So Golden Gardens remains as an almost typical Puget Sound beach, even though readily accessible within the city.

This simple scene on Foster Island along the edge of Union Bay, previously sketched for the 1962 *Seattle Cityscape*, was sketched again for the present book. Although recognizable from the earlier scene, the place has been violated by the second Lake Washington floating expressway, seen in the right middle distance and only a few hundred yards away. People continue to enjoy coming here for the stroll and to look across the water, even though the constant roar and vibration of the transgressing auto traffic is inescapable. The swamp still harbors natural life, although it is no longer an effective wildlife sanctuary. Highways can go anywhere, but civilization cannot replace areas such as this. The disruption of Union Bay and Foster Island is a serious loss for the city. Even as deterioration of so many of the city's attributes continues, the optimist retains hope that these outrages will serve as object lessons in bringing about increased civic enlightenment and necessary effective citizen action.

Mount Rainier—no matter what happens, Mount Rainier will always be there!
Until a highway is built to the top, there will always be a place to escape to.
The Mountain has a message for every citizen as an expression of the glory
of nature, of the wilderness, of scenic splendor, of outdoor recreation, and of
the availability and indestructibility of these things and many more. Seattle was
laid out by the gods so that everyone would be aware of the existence of that
large heap of stone and snow. When the Mountain is "out," all is well with
the world, and Seattleites are cheered and refreshed by its splendor. For many
its reality is a symbolic reason for living in Seattle.

Index

ACKNOWLEDGMENTS

Thanks are tendered to the following for the use of drawings: the Special Collections of the University of Washington Libraries and its curator Robert C. Monroe; George Bartholick; the Bumgardner Partnership; Richard Haag Associates; the Richardson Associates; Peter Staten; Dr. and Mrs. Milan V. Starks; and Matthew, David, and Peter Steinbrueck. Special appreciation is given to the people of the University of Washington Press for their tolerance and helpfulness in all ways; and to my wife, Marjorie, for her more than considerable assistance and understanding.